C0-ALR-119

What's Saddam Hussein's favorite laxative?
(see page 9)

What do Air Force flight simulators and *Playboy* have in common?
(see page 17)

What do you call a four-foot woman in the Navy?
(see page 24)

What's the difference between a prophylactic and an Army-issue parachute?
(see page 53)

What's the new Iraqi Army flag?
(see page 67)

What do Saddam Hussein and pantyhose have in common?
(see page 82)

Also by Blanche Knott
Published by St. Martin's Press

Blanche Knott's

Truly
Tasteless
Military
Jokes

ST. MARTIN'S PAPERBACKS

TRULY TASTELESS MILITARY JOKES

Copyright © 1991 by Blanche Knott.

ISBN: 0-312-92726-6

Printed in the United States of America

St. Martin's Paperbacks edition/August 1991

10 9 8 7 6 5 4 3 2 1

to the men and women
who served in Operation Desert Shield and Storm

On the eve of battle, a private stationed in Saudi Arabia got a letter from his fiancée. He expected the usual litany of sensible advice, but instead the message was only eight words: "Kick theirs, cover yours, kiss mine, Love, Donna."

•

Why are they sending so many women with PMS to the Gulf?

They love to pick fights, and they retain water for four days.

•

The Navy computer was programmed to converse on a level with the IQ entered by the programmer. When 190 was punched in, the computer began a discussion of the Big Bang theory and its cosmological implications. 140 resulted in a lively discussion of the trade deficit and its effect on the strength of the dollar in world markets. At 110, the computer produced its candidates for the starting lineup of the next World Series. And at 55, the computer began to sing, "From the halls of Montezuma . . ."

●

Did you hear the Army has developed an elite Special Forces commando group composed entirely of Hispanic soldiers?

In case of war, they're dropped behind enemy lines to strip the armored vehicles.

●

The buck private served under a sadistic sergeant, who gave him latrine duty so many days in a row that he decided he had to get out of the Army on a Section Eight. The next day found him with latrine duty once again. He scrubbed until the whole room was hospital clean, then took a big gob of peanut butter and stuck it on the last toilet seat.

"What's that?" growled the sergeant, delighted to have found something to get on the soldier's case about. "Looks like shit, doesn't it, asswipe?"

The private came over, scooped up some of the stuff on his finger, and popped it right in his mouth. "Well, sir," he reported thoughtfully, "it sure ain't piss."

•

Why do women flock around Army sharpshooters?
They've got a reputation as crack shots.

•

The wolf whistle stopped the two attractive officers in their tracks. "I'll handle this," the captain ordered her lieutenant, then turned to pin the stammering soldier against the side of the barracks. At the top of her voice she treated him to a lecture on women's rights, military protocol, and his general lack of fitness for membership in the human race, let alone the Marine Corps. "Have you anything to say for yourself?" she concluded contemptuously.

"Nope," quavered the soldier, "only that I wasn't whistling at you, sir."

The young sergeant was selected by her commanding officer to take part in an intensive leadership-training course, which required a six-week stint roughing it in the wilderness. Her first letter home to her best friend reported the exciting news that she had met a guy on the program that she really liked. "But since we aren't allowed to wear make-up," the letter continued, "he has no idea what I really look like."

•

Did you hear about the medic-alert dog tags worn by epileptic blacks in the service?

They say, "I Am Not Break Dancing."

•

The sergeant put his troops through a fancy drill, at the end of which they lined up three rows deep. Walking down the line, the sergeant stopped in front of each soldier, whacked him on the chest with his baton, and barked, "Did that hurt, soldier?"

"No, *sir!*" each replied.

"Why not?" yelled the sergeant.

"Because I'm a United States Marine, *sir!*" came the reply.

Continuing on, the sergeant saw a huge penis sticking out of the line and proceeded to whack it with his baton. "Did that hurt, soldier?" he boomed.

"No, *sir*," answered the private.

"And why not?"

"Because it belongs to the guy behind me, *sir!*"

•

Define "indiscreet":

Where a black motorpool sergeant parks the Company Jeep.

•

The incredibly handsome GI came into the PX and asked if they stocked Valentines. The blushing clerk showed him to the display and offered a suggestion. "This one's my favorite—it says, 'To the only girl I'll ever love.' "

"Great," he agreed. "I'll take a dozen and a pack of Trojans."

•

The British officer was not particularly pleased when he was assigned to a detachment of American soldiers in a NATO post, and his worst fears were confirmed when the American officer in charge came over and slapped him on the back. "Hey there, Nigel," the American boomed, "call me Biff. You're going to like our camp," he went on heartily. "We don't just sit around watching the grass grow and waiting for orders, you know. Take Monday nights. On Mondays we all get drunk as skunks."

"Count me out," said the Englishman stiffly. "I don't drink."

"Hey, pal, that's okay," the American reassured him. "You'll have some fun on Tuesday nights when we all get wrecked on weed."

"I wouldn't think of it, old sport."

"Not to worry," the American officer continued, "because you'll love Wednesdays. That's when we bring the local chicks over and the real fun begins."

"I hate to disappoint you, old chap," said Nigel, "but I do not consort with cheap women."

"You don't?" The American was clearly puzzled. "Say, you aren't one of those queers, are you?"

"Certainly not!" retorted the Brit, highly insulted.

Biff whistled through his teeth. "Well, for sure you're not gonna like Thursday nights."

.

What's the worst tile to hear called out in a Baghdad Bingo game?

"B-52!"

●

Henderson had been a track-and-field star in high school, and his worst nightmare came true when he was felled by some shrapnel and woke up in the hospital to find his lower legs a shapeless mass of plaster and gauze. The doctor confirmed his worst fears, informing him that both legs had been amputated below the knee. "I'm terribly sorry, Sergeant Henderson—we tried to save them," the doctor assured him. "But I do have some good news."

"Jesus, Doc, I could sure use it," said the white-faced soldier.

"See that guy in the bed over there?" The doctor gestured across the aisle and Henderson nodded feebly. "Well, he'd like to buy your boots."

●

Know why all the Greek soldiers were wearing black armbands last month?

Didn't you hear about the ship that went down with ten thousand cases of Vaseline?

Three infantrymen were captured by Iraqi forces behind enemy lines and summarily sentenced to be executed by a firing squad at dawn. The next morning, as twelve gun barrels were leveled at MacGowan, he screamed, "Tornado!" The firing squad fell to the ground and in the ensuing confusion MacGowan got away.

Next came Kostolian's turn to face the firing squad. At the last second he screamed, "Sandstorm!" And while the Iraqis dropped their weapons to cover their faces, he got away.

Wojcik had paid close attention and decided to give the same method a try. The last to be hauled before the firing squad, he took a deep breath and yelled, "Fire!"

•

Did you hear about the new Israeli Army doll for girls?

It's called GI JAP.

An Air National Guard captain was being interviewed by a group of high-ranking officers for a full-time position at an Air Guard base. His technical competence was clear, but, wanting to make sure the fellow would get along with their tight-knit group, one colonel asked, "And do you play golf?"

The captain's reply clinched his appointment. "No, sir, but I caddy."

•

What's Saddam Hussein's favorite laxative?

The U.S. Air Force. When those planes bombed his bunker, he *shat*.

•

Lieutenant Dawson had wanted to be an astronaut since age three, so he was thrilled when NASA admitted him to its training program, and even more excited when in due course he was selected as the astronaut for the first manned Army mission to Mars.

"Not to worry, Dawson," his superior officer informed him condescendingly. "Every function aboard the capsule will be completely automated—flight plan, navigation, data transmissions, satellite operations, the works. All you have to do is wave to the folks every so often, and pee in the little plastic bags.

Got it?" Dawson was a little miffed, but since he didn't want to be passed over, he just acknowledged the instructions with a nod.

On the day of the launch, Lieutenant Dawson was duly strapped in and blasted into orbit. He was watching the curve of the Earth disappear behind the booster rocket when he was startled by a mechanized voice coming over his headphones. "Welcome aboard, Lieutenant Dawson," urged the disembodied voice, "and enjoy the latest development in military reconnaissance technology. Your flight will be completely controlled by the latest, state-of-the-art instrumentation. Air composition and pressure is monitored continuously; course corrections processed by the computer five times every second; meals will be served by a robotic arm and waste bags collected via the same mechanism. So just lean back, relax, and enjoy the view, confident in the knowledge that nothing whatsoever can go wrong . . . go wrong . . . go wrong . . ."

•

"I think the new medic's a crackpot," confessed Corporal Meyers to Staff Sergeant Stokowski. "I went to see him about my piles, and he told me to drink carrot juice after a hot bath."

"You never know," commented Stokowski. "How'd the carrot juice taste?"

"Don't know yet; I've only drunk half the bath so far."

•

Why did General Santa Ana only send 10,000 men to attack the Alamo?
He only had two cars.

•

The young lieutenant fresh out of OCS headed up a group of recruits to pitch tents. After giving them the correct interval, the lieutenant hesitated, realizing he had forgotten the correct command. Finally, in desperation, he called out loudly, "Build little houses . . . build!"

•

The instructor had just spent an hour drilling the recruits in the basics of guard duty, so when the first man on duty thoroughly blew it, he was furious. "You failed to challenge your intruder for a password," he bellowed, *"and* you neglected to request proper identification. Are you deaf, or just too stupid to remember two things at once?"

"I'm sorry, sir," the soldier explained sheepishly, "but I was positive it was Private Hill. She's the only one in the platoon who wears Chanel No. 5."

•

How can you spot the gay Special Forces man at the beach?

By the shaving scars on his legs.

•

Responding to desperate hand signals from the soldier on the operating table, the Army nurse bent over to catch his urgent whisper. The surgeon was startled when she turned and gently but firmly took hold of the scalpel before he could begin the incision.

"Excuse me, Major," the nurse explained with a blush, "but the patient would like to know what you were in private life."

•

Why does Paris have so many tree-lined boulevards? So the German Army could march in the shade.

•

Read the new Soviet bestseller?
Cream of the Russian Army by Ivan Jackinoff.

•

The Ecuadorian captain had grown increasingly anxious over rumors of an impending air strike from neighboring Peru. "Pedro," he ordered his aide-de-camp, "I want you to climb that mountain and report any signs of Peruvian military activity."

"Si, Capitano," replied Pedro. He obediently trudged up the mountain, and as soon as he crossed the ridge he spotted a squadron of planes heading their way. "There are many planes coming, Capitano," he promptly radioed back.

"Friends or enemies?" the captain demanded urgently.

Pedro again lifted his binoculars to the sky. "They're flying very closely together, Capitano," he reported. "I think they must be friends."

•

Did you hear about the tragic war between the Poles and the Germans?

The Poles threw dynamite, and the Germans lit it and threw it back.

•

Vessels of the American Navy say "U.S.S.", which stands for "United States Ship". Vessels of the British Navy say "H.M.S.", which stands for "Her Majesty's Ship." Vessels of the Italian Navy say "A.M.B." Know what that stands for?

"Atsa My Boat!"

•

Two none-too-bright sailors went into San Diego for a wild night. They took two obliging hookers back to their hotel room, where things proceeded to heat up. At this point the girls provided them with condoms, explaining that they protected against AIDS, VD, and herpes.

A couple of hours after the girls had left, one sailor poked the other. "Sal," he asked sleepily, "do you really care if those girls get the clap?"

"Naw," Jake mumbled.

"So let's take these damn things off—I have to take a wicked piss!"

•

Japanese woman to GI (lowering the top of her kimono): "Nipponese! Nipponese!"
Chinese woman to GI (pulling down her pants): "Chu Manchu! Chu Manchu!"

•

Two privates assigned to guard duty in a remote mountain outpost grew lonelier and hornier by the day. Jimmy, who'd grown up on a farm, confessed he'd been eyeing the sheep grazing on a nearby hillside. "The trick," he confessed to his buddy, "is to sneak up behind her, grab ahold of her rear legs, spread 'em and lift 'em up to your crotch."

"That sounds easy enough," admitted the other soldier, "but how do you kiss her?"

•

What do you call a truckload of vibrators delivered to the WAC barracks?
    Toys for twats.

•

Six ROTC officer candidates decided to rent an off-campus house together. They couldn't afford anything fancy, and it didn't take long for them to detect that their new home was infested by rats. So, armed with baseball bats and any other weapons they could get their hands on, they went down to the basement one night to do battle with their unwelcome guests.

Three weeks later, having failed to raise any of his tenants by telephone, the landlord used his key to enter the house. Finding only one badly beaten man, he cried, "Good God, what happened? And where are the other five?"

"Two were killed in action," croaked the battered fellow, "and the other three ran off with war brides."

•

Why did the Panamanian tank cruise around the block forty-eight times?

His blinker got stuck.

•

The troop ship had been at sea for many weeks when the troubled boatswain's mate paid a visit to the captain's cabin. "I think there's unnatural sex going on aboard this ship, Captain," he informed him. Telling him to come back when he had proof, the captain sternly dismissed him.

A few days later the mate came forward with the same accusation and again the captain brushed off the charges for lack of evidence. So he was rather startled when the empty-handed mate came to speak to him a third time.

"I must insist on proof," he reprimanded the sailor.

"But Captain," blurted the mate unhappily, "this is the third time I've tasted shit on the chief petty officer's prick!"

•

What do Air Force flight simulators and *Playboy* have in common?

They both improve hand-eye coordination.

•

At mail call, Ensign Smith was delighted to be handed a big envelope from his wife, but rather puzzled by the intricate drawing it contained. At the bottom he found his wife had scrawled a brief note. "This is how our dashboard looks," it read. "Do we need oil?"

Why don't gay soldiers lean on their M16s?

They're afraid it might get too serious.

•

During the Indian Wars a cavalry brigade led a charge against a tribe of Cheyenne warriors, completely decimating the Indians. At the end the only one left alive was the Indian chief. "Since you fought so bravely," said the cavalry officer, "I'm going to spare your life."

Just as the chief was trying to find words to express his gratitude, over the hill came a mess of Indians who completely wiped out the cavalry brigade. The only survivor was the officer, to whom the Indian said, "I'm not going to be as generous as you were—you're going to die. But you can have three wishes before I kill you."

The officer nodded, thought for a minute, and said, "I'd like to see my horse." The horse was brought around, the officer whispered in its ear, and the horse tore off, only to return in an hour or so with a luscious blonde on its back.

"Please feel free to make use of my tepee," offered the chief tactfully. When the officer emerged some time later, the chief asked about his second wish.

"I'd like to see my horse." Again the horse received a whispered command and galloped off, this time returning with a lovely redhead. Again the chief gestured graciously toward his tepee, and again waited an appropriate amount of time before inquiring as to his prisoner's last wish.

"I'd like to see my horse." This time when the horse was led up to him, the officer grasped its bridle firmly, pinched its lips with his other hand, and whispered fiercely, "Watch my lips—I said *posse.*"

•

What do you do when an Iraqi tank is mounting an assault on you?

Shoot the guy pushing it.

•

Leroy and Jasper have just been promoted from privates to sergeants. Not long after, they're out for a walk and Leroy says, "Hey Jasper, there's the NCO Club. Let's you and me stop in."

"But we're privates," protests Jasper.

"We're sergeants now," says Leroy, pulling him inside. "Now Jasper, I'm gonna sit down and have me a drink."

"But we're privates," says Jasper.

"You blind?" asks Leroy, waving his stripes in his

buddy's face. "We're sergeants now." So they have their drink, and pretty soon a hooker comes up to Leroy.

"You're cute," she says, "and I'd like to screw you but I've got a bad case of gonorrhea."

Leroy pulls his friend to the side and whispers, "Jasper, go look in the dictionary and see what that 'gonorrhea' means. If it's OK, give me the OK sign." So Jasper goes to look it up, comes back, and gives Leroy the big thumbs-up.

Three weeks later Leroy is laid up in the infirmary with a terrible case of gonorrhea. "Jasper," he says, "what the hell you give me an OK for?"

"Well, Leroy, in the dictionary, it say gonorrhea affects only the privates." Jasper points to his stripes. "But we're sergeants now."

•

A destroyer was sunk in an engagement with a Japanese submarine, leaving the captain and seven of his crew adrift in a lifeboat. After two weeks at sea, supplies were running low and the captain decided that instead of having them all starve to death, he would shoot himself and let the men eat his body. As he put the loaded revolver to his temple, a young gunnery second mate begged, "Oh Captain, Captain, don't shoot yourself in the head."

"I have to do what I have to do, my boy," the captain explained gently.

"But you don't understand, sir," said the sailor. "Brains are my favorite dish."

•

Sergeant Mack had a fine time during his stay in Hong Kong, but paid for it when he came down with a strange Oriental venereal disease. After making the rounds of every American doctor in the community, to his horror he discovered that not only were they unable to cure him, but each informed him that the only remedy was to have his penis amputated.

Desperate, Sergeant Mack made an appointment with a leading Chinese doctor, figuring that he might know more about an Eastern malady. "Do you, Doctor Chung, think I need to have my dick amputated?" he asked anxiously.

"No, no, no," said the Chinese doctor testily.

A huge smile broke out over the serviceman's face. "Boy, that's *great,* Doc. Every one of those American medics said they'd have to cut it off."

"Those Western doctors—all they ever want to do is cut, cut, cut," explained Dr. Chung in exasperation. "You just wait two weeks. Penis fall off all by itself."

•

Medic at dispensary: What's that on your shoulder, soldier?

GI: A birthmark, sir.

Medic: Hmmm. How long have you had it?

•

The non-com whose job consisted of shuffling papers from eight-thirty to four-thirty every day found an excellent way to reduce bothersome interruptions. She posted a sign above her desk which read, I HAVEN'T SEEN IT.

•

If our ancestors came over on a boat, how did herpes get here?

On the Captain's dinghy.

•

Why don't sergeants give Puerto Rican work crews more than half an hour for lunch?

They don't want to have to retrain them.

Did you hear about the masochistic Marine sergeant who drilled his privates?

•

The two men from the Quartermaster Corps got a little leave and were taking a walk on the beach when a sea gull unloaded on the first man's shoulder.

"Too bad," his buddy commiserated. "You want me to get some toilet paper?"

"Nah," he replied with a shrug. "It's probably a mile away by now."

•

President Bush was returning in Air Force One from a trip to Berlin when the pilot advised him that they were putting down at Homestead A.F.B. for about twenty minutes to refuel. Deciding to take the opportunity to stretch his legs and take a leak, Bush walked over to the latrine and found himself at a urinal next to a very large black sergeant. Unable to resist comment, the President asked, "Say, Sergeant, how in the hell do you get one that big?"

"It's easy enough, suh," said the sergeant. "You

puts it in easy, you takes it out easy, and you jus' keeps it up—that's all there is to it."

The President could hardly wait till all the welcoming ceremonies were over with at the White House before trying out his newfound rhythm on Barbara. But after a couple of easy ins and easy outs, she sat up and exclaimed, "George, for God's sake—will you quit screwing like a black man?!"

•

What do you call a four-foot woman in the Navy?
    A microWAVE.

•

Flight instructions were to pick up the Navy commander and bring him back to the aircraft carrier stationed in the Mediterranean. In an effort to reassure the passenger in mid-flight, the pilot turned and asked, "Sir, is this your first carrier landing in a jet fighter?"

In reply, the commander opened his inflatable vest to show a chestful of medals, and said disdainfully, "Son, I've made so many carrier landings I've lost count. At least three hundred fifty."

"Oh, good," said the pilot without missing a beat, " 'cause this is my first."

What's the room called where enlisted women give the officers blowjobs?

Headquarters.

⦁

The American pilot finally downed the Messerschmidt, but was so impressed with the German's flying skill that he went to visit him in the field hospital. Finding the fellow in pretty bad shape, the American asked if he could do anything for him.

The Nazi admitted that he did have a favor to ask. "The leg they amputated . . . on your next bombing run, could you drop it over the Fatherland?"

"Sure, pal." It was a pretty weird request but the pilot was happy to oblige, and came back to tell him the mission had been carried out.

The grateful German gasped his thanks, and another request. "The other leg got very bad, they had to cut it off. Could this, too, be dropped over my homeland? It would mean a great deal to me."

The American shrugged, but returned two days later with the news that the job was done. "Many thanks," whispered the downed Nazi, now ashen-faced and unable to lift his head from the pillow. "I have just one final request. Last night they had to amputate my right arm—"

"Now hang on just a darn minute," interrupted the American angrily. "Are you trying to escape?"

•

Who was the dumbest soldier in history?

The one who wrote *Stars & Stripes* demanding the identity of the Unknown Soldier.

•

The Australian chief petty officer couldn't wait for shore leave in the Big Apple. He lost no time in picking up a hooker and bringing her back to his hotel room. Asking her to undress, he proceeded to lean the bed up against the wall and toss every other article of furniture out the window, down the airshaft.

"What on earth are you planning to do with me?" asked the hooker nervously.

"I'm not exactly sure, ma'am," answered the Australian, "but if it's anything like it is with a kangaroo, we'll need all the room we can get."

•

Did you hear about the gay private who put shoe polish in his Vaseline . . .

. . . so he could rise and shine?

•

The gunner's mate went into the PX and asked for the most reliable aphrodisiac available. "I got a couple of Navy nurses coming over this weekend and they're gonna be horny as hell," he whispered across the counter. "I wanna be able to handle them all myself, know what I mean?"

The pharmacist handed him a little jar with a conspiratorial wink, and wished him a happy weekend.

Monday morning the mate crawled into the PX and croaked, "Ben Gay . . . I need some Ben Gay."

For your pecker?" asked the incredulous pharmacist. "It'll sting like hell."

"No, for my elbow. The women didn't show."

•

The orderly's duties included bringing the colonel a cup of coffee at six o'clock every morning, and every morning the colonel was enraged because the coffee cup arrived two-thirds full. None of the officer's insults and fits of rage produced a full cup of coffee, until he threatened the fellow with a full month of KP duty.

The next morning he was greeted with a cup of coffee full to the brim, and the morning after that, and the morning after that. Finally the colonel couldn't resist smugly complimenting the orderly on his mastery of the new technique.

"Oh, there's nothing much to it, sir," admitted the fellow cheerfully. "I take some coffee in my mouth outside the mess hall, and spit it back in right outside your door."

•

Hear about the Irish sailor who wanted to be buried at sea?

His two sons died digging the grave.

•

Commanding officer: "Why aren't you working?"
Private: "I didn't see you coming, sir."

•

It's the middle of the night when the spacecraft lands in the middle of a deserted Iowa cornfield. The Martian battalion—the aliens look kind of like your average gas pump, not exactly but pretty close—descend from the ship and begin looking for signs of intelligent life. Coming across a road in close formation, they follow it until they encounter a one-pump gas station, which looks somewhat like a Martian—not exactly, but pretty close.

This must be what they are seeking! Ordering his men to fall out and take cover, the Martian captain comes forward cautiously and addresses the pumps. "Greetings. We come from Mars in search of intelligent beings. Will you take us to your leader?" When there's no response, he repeats his query as loudly as possible. Still no answer, so he turns to his voice translator. Finally, enraged by the lack of a reply, he whips out his laser gun and points it at the pump. "Why you insolent son-of-a-glukfarb—take us to your leader or I'll blast you!" His lieutenant tries to stop him, but it's too late. The captain fires, and an immense explosion hurls the Martians a hundred feet in the air.

Three hours later they come to. As the lieutenant helps him to his feet, the captain asks shakily, "Wha . . . what happened? Did the enemy return fire?"

The lieutenant replies, "Look captain, if I told you once, I told you a hundred times: you just don't go messing with a soldier who can wrap his prick twice around his waist and stick it in his ear."

At his Navy induction the nervous recruit was handed a medical form, which asked, "Do you have or have you ever had any of the following disorders?" In his confusion, the recruit checked almost all of them "yes."

When he reached the head of the line, the doctor, a full commander, looked the questionnaire over and bellowed, "You don't need a physical, you moron—you need an autopsy."

•

Did you hear about the gay sperm whale recruited by the enemy?

He bit the head off a submarine and swallowed all the seamen.

•

M. P. Monroe's mother couldn't wait for her first visit to the Air Force base in Nevada where he'd been stationed. Dutifully he showed her around and answered her many questions—except one about where the road behind the mess hall led. He ignored the question a second time, which was enough for his mother to launch into a lecture about good manners, respecting one's elders—

"Mom," Monroe interrupted, "lay off, will you? If I tell you, I'll have to shoot you."

•

What do you call this? [Hold up a twisted paper clip.]
   A Green Beret's pubic hair.

•

The fighting on the front lines was fierce. Marshalling his troops, the commanding officer yelled over the thunder of artillery, "The Germans are coming! Men, they outnumber us four to one, so each of you must do his job and do it well."

A rawboned GI from Kentucky proceeded to blaze away for five minutes or so. Then he put his gun down and proceeded to pick calmly at his teeth.

"What's wrong, soldier?" asked the officer, running over.

The Kentuckian drawled, "Got my four."

•

The Special Forces commando had commandeered a Kuwaiti camel for a special mission, but suddenly the beast stopped dead in its tracks. Despite a stream of physical and verbal abuse, the camel refused to take another step. The fellow was just standing there, cursing furiously, when a jeep appeared over the crest of the sand dune. "What's the problem?" asked the WAC at the wheel.

"My camel won't go," admitted the embarrassed commando.

The WAC jumped out, reached between the camel's rear legs for a moment—and the animal took off like a shot.

"Impressive," he conceded. "What did you do?"

"Just tickled his testicles," she replied with a grin. "Works every time."

The commando turned his back, dropped his pants, and said, "Well, you better tickle mine, 'cause I've gotta catch him!"

●

What's the definition of an Army barbershop?

A place where you wait at least two hours for a haircut that takes less than two minutes.

●

The airman third class came in to the squadron's commanding officer with a complaint of long standing. "Captain, the first sergeant is really out to get me," he began. "He gets on my case about every damn thing I do, puts me on detail all the time, always pushes me to the limit. Sir, I wouldn't be surprised if he orders me to jump in the latrine."

"Well, if he does," responded the captain, "report to me immediately, understand?"

"Yes, sir," replied the airman, a big smile spreading across his face.

It froze, however, when the captain elaborated, "But Hinckley—you'd better smell like shit."

•

Why does the Mexican Army's chihuahua mascot have a snubbed nose?

From chasing parked tanks.

•

It was just before a critical offensive, and the Polish troops were being issued their weapons. Lenski was last in line, and they handed out the last rifle to the man in front of him. Furious, Lenski shouted, "Hey, what about my gun?"

"Listen, bud," advised the munitions officer, "just

keep your hands out in front of you as though you were holding one, and yell, 'Bang! Bang!' "

"You gotta be joking," blustered Lenski. "You must be trying to get me killed!"

"Trust me," said the officer, sending Lenski out into the field with a reassuring pat on the shoulder.

Pretty soon Lenski found himself in the thick of battle with a Russian infantryman advancing on him. Having little choice, he raised his hands, pointed at the soldier, and yelled, "Bang! Bang!" The Russian fell over, stone dead. This worked on about twenty Russians. Fired with confidence, Lenski returned to the munitions officer and asked about a bayonet.

"Oh, we're all out," said the officer apologetically, "but if you just point with your index finger and scream, 'Stab! Stab!' you'll get excellent results."

Out went Lenski into battle again, and soon he was surrounded by heaps of dead Russian soldiers. In fact, he thought he had wiped out the whole platoon, and was just taking a breather when he saw a giant Russian coming towards him. Strutting forward, Lenski shouted, "Bang! Bang!"

The Russian kept on coming.

"Stab! Stab!" cried Lenski.

The Russian kept on coming, right over Lenski, crushing him to a pulp. The last thing the unfortunate infantryman heard was the Russian muttering, "Tank, tank, tank. . . ."

•

The woman came into the Red Cross Blood Center and explained that since her husband and brother were stationed in the Gulf, she wanted to donate blood. "And I want it to go to the Iraqis," she instructed.

"Why on earth . . . ?" asked the puzzled technician.

"I have hepatitis," she explained with a smile.

•

Do you know why they won't let Puerto Rican pilots fly the Stealth Bomber?

They'd honk the horn, squeal the tires, and play the radio too damn loud.

•

After three long months of boot camp chow, the recruit couldn't wait for his first pass to town. Dashing into the first place he saw, he ordered a turkey platter with roast potatoes and peas. "And for dessert, a big piece of apple pie, à la mode," he finished breathlessly.

"Sonny, you must have just gotten out of boot camp," the woman behind the counter remarked kindly.

"Gee, how could you tell?" wondered the GI. "Is that what everyone orders?"

"No. Because this is a beauty parlor."

•

First soldier: "Why'd you break off your engagement?"

Second soldier: "Had to. She wanted to get married."

•

What's six miles long and goes four miles an hour?

An Iraqi Army convoy with only one set of jumper cables.

•

After an endless day of grueling maneuvers under the blazing Georgia sun, the platoon stood wearily in formation in front of the barracks. "All right, you pathetic lumps of flab, think about this," bellowed the drill instructor. "If you could have fifteen minutes alone, right now, with anyone in the world, who would it be?"

Amid the sighs of longing, a voice spoke up from the back row: "My recruiter."

•

Why do Hispanic soldiers install small steering wheels in their tanks?
It makes it easier to drive with handcuffs on.

•

What kind of military gossip's the most lethal?
The kind you hear through the carbine.

•

The recent recruit was on guard at the main gate of a key Naval base, and was given strict orders to admit absolutely no cars which had not been issued a special new permit. Finally the inevitable happened: the recruit stopped a car containing a high-ranking officer.

"Drive on," ordered the admiral, dismissing the guard with a wave.

"I'm sorry, sir, but I'm new at this," admitted the recruit, drawing a deep breath. "Who do I shoot—you or your driver?"

Did you hear about the dim major who died . . .
. . . and left his money to the Unknown Soldier's widow?

•

The Naval officer took a walk around his ship, surveying his men at work readying the flagship for its next tour of duty. Off the bow, a crew on a scaffold was busy scraping and painting. Looking down into their sweaty, paint-spattered faces, the officer called out, "What're you doing, sailors?"

Wiping the expression of disbelief off his face, one quick-witted midshipman quickly answered, "Thinking about re-enlisting, sir."

•

What's green, yellow, purple, blue, orange, and red?
An Italian soldier all dressed up.

•

The young second lieutenant out on a date with a gorgeous redhead ran into his CO. "Uh, this is my sister, sir," he stammered.

"That's OK, Lieutenant," said the CO graciously. "She used to be mine."

•

What's the definition of an optimist?

Someone who makes out a duty roster in ink.

•

The little guy was already the victim of much abuse from his platoon members, but the crowning insult occurred one night in a particularly filthy and bed-bug-infested barracks. Amidst the general scratching, slapping, and cursing, a plaintive wail was heard from the direction of Joey's bunk: "Put me down, you little shits!"

•

How can you spot a bull dyke in the Special Forces?

She kick starts her vibrator and rolls her own tampons.

Inspecting officer: Soldier, your rifle is dirty—take a look!

Private: That's OK, sir, I'll take your word for it.

●

Ordered to knock out an enemy machine-gun nest single-handedly, Ranger Pfc. LaGuardia began to tremble violently.

"What are you nervous about?" barked the corporal.

"N-n-not a thing, sir," stammered LaGuardia. "I'm just shaking from patriotism."

●

Reporter to soldier stationed in West Germany: "And how do you manage your salary?"

GI with arm around pretty *fräulein:* "Oh, I spend most of it maintaining civilian morale."

●

The flight surgeon happened to be a gynecologist, which made him the butt of endless jokes from the squadron. Delighted when his tour of duty came to an end, he was even more pleased to be able to announce that his replacement had the perfect medical background to deal with a bunch of assholes.

"Dr. Houseman," he informed them with a grin, "is a proctologist."

•

Overheard in the mess hall: "Hey, great meat! It's so tender you can cut it with your knife."

•

Upon completing his Army Airborne training, Hawkins was granted leave. He was waiting for his train when a teenager, clearly impressed, came over to him.

"I'm off to basic training," he informed Hawkins shyly. Then, catching sight of the Airborne wings pinned to the dress greens, the kid exclaimed, "Wow! You actually jumped out of a plane, didn't you?"

Modesty got the better of the recent graduate. "Nah," Hawkins admitted with a shrug. "I was pushed five times."

Did you hear McDonald-Douglas just developed the first vasectomy procedure approved by the Pentagon?

The only problem is that if you get a hard-on, your dick falls off.

•

The GI was summoned to his CO's office for a slight infraction of the rules. He exited a minute later, muttering, "Geez, that son-of-a-bitch sure is tight with words. He said, 'Come in, Sergeant. Sit down, Sergeant. Stand up, Private. Good day, Private.' "

•

Did you hear that things were getting so tough at the recruiting centers . . .

. . . they started accepting midgets pasted together?

•

Pfc in strange mess hall contemplating the hash: "What's in it?"

Hash slinger: "Relax—no one you know."

•

One of the questions put to the candidate at his OCS exam was, "Where is the Suwannee River?"

The young man thought for a moment, then wrote, "Far, far away."

He passed.

•

The Air Force captain and his wife, a sergeant, were in the habit of having dinner Friday night at the Officer's Club. One evening a new couple joined them at the table, and the woman lost no time in making her status as a captain's wife crystal-clear. "Our last post was dreadful," she soon confided. "Why, we had to live right next door to those *enlisted* people."

The Air Force captain nodded sympathetically, leaned over, and whispered loudly, "You think that's bad? I have to *sleep* with one."

•

The two sardines were swimming aimlessly around San Diego Bay when one suggested they go up to San Francisco for the weekend. "It's too far to swim," complained the second fish.

"We could take the train," suggested the first sardine good-naturedly.

"What—and be crammed in like soldiers?"

•

Saudi dignitary visiting US base in the Gulf: "Why do all the American soldiers look so cheerful?"
GI: "Because we get to go back to the States; you have to live here."

•

The small-town Mom was shocked by her homesick son's tales of the horrors of boot camp, especially by his descriptions of how the drill sergeant singled him out for abuse, yelling at him for being ugly, thick-headed, fat, dumb, and a generally worthless specimen of American sissyhood.

"Aw, honey, that's terrible," she sympathized. "Now why on earth would he want to say such false, unkind things about my big, brave boy?"

"I dunno, Mom," moaned the miserable recruit. "And you should hear what he says about you!"

Why did the DI marry his dog?

He had to.

•

By late afternoon it was clear that the platoon was outnumbered and outflanked, and the first lieutenant decided it was time for a little pep talk. "Keep on fighting, boys," he began grandly, "until the last shot is fired. Then run."

He cleared his throat and looked about. "I'm a little lame, so I'm starting now."

•

Did you hear about the special juke box for soldiers with battle fatigue?

You put in a quarter and get five minutes of silence.

•

The Marine Corps lance corporal insisted he needed a new pair of glasses and that he didn't have time to wait for an appointment, but his pleas fell on deaf ears. He was heading for the door when a two-star general entered the clinic. The warrant officer snapped to attention with a "Good afternoon, Colonel!"

"Get that dumb bastard some glasses!" yelled the general.

The lance corporal was shown right in.

•

Why were there so many black casualties in Vietnam?

Because every time the sergeant yelled, "Get down!" they stood up and danced.

•

The brand new second lieutenant was eager that his platoon's inspection go smoothly. Everything was proceeding according to plan until the inspector general paused in front of a particularly thick-headed soldier and asked him his job.

"I rake leaves, sir," was his reply.

"No, soldier," said the inspector kindly. "I mean, what would you do in wartime?"

"Uh . . . sir, I'd rake faster."

What do you get when you cross a chicken with an NCO?

Pecking orders.

•

Concerned that the men on watch stay alert during routine patrols in the Persian Gulf, the commanding officer had the following sign pasted on the foredeck: ANY SHIP CAN BE A MINESWEEPER—ONCE.

•

At a fund-raising auction for an Air Force unit, the high bidder won the right to throw a pie in the face of the officer or NCO of his choice. When a chief master sergeant known across the base as a real son-of-a-bitch was persuaded to step onto the block, the bidding was fast and furious. However, it was his wife whose bid of eighty-five dollars landed a chocolate cream pie in the sergeant's face.

"Anything else I can do for you?" the sergeant snarled as he wiped the whipped cream out of his eyes.

"Yes, honey, there is," his wife informed him sweetly. "I need to borrow seventy-five dollars."

•

What does U.S. ARMY stand for?
Uncle Sam Ain't Released Me Yet.

•

Three soldiers, one American, one French, and one British, went on leave together and decided to blow some of their back pay on a really fancy meal. The best restaurant in town boasted four specials of the day: Barbecued American, for $6.75; Pan-fried Frenchman, for $8.50; Baked Brit, for $9.95; and Broiled Arab, for $21.00.

"Quite a price difference," the Frenchman commented. "Is the Arab especially delicious?"

"No, they all taste pretty much the same," replied the waiter candidly.

"Then why's the dish so expensive? There must be a reason," persisted the Frenchman.

"Oh there is, there is. Have you any idea how long it takes to clean an Arab?"

•

During a parachuting exercise, the Green Beret jumped out over the drop area but was forced by a twenty-one-knot wind to land on a nearby golf course. He fumbled for the release, but a big gust drove the chute along the fairway, pulling the struggling soldier along.

"Need any help?" called out a couple of golfers who'd observed his plight.

"No thanks," the soldier called out gamely as he slid past. "I'll just play through."

•

What do you call a military engagement between two test-tube babies?

Jar Wars!

•

Returning to base late after a weekend leave, the soldier was hustling back to her quarters when the sentry called out, "Halt! Who goes there?"

Obediently, she stopped in her tracks and gave him her name, rank, serial number, and Army unit. A long pause followed. Finally she inquired rather timidly, "Aren't you supposed to say something else?"

"Yes!" barked the guard. "And don't move a goddamn inch until I remember what."

•

"How long have you been in the Navy, son?" asked the admiral of the young sailor at the radar screen.

"Six weeks—and you, sir?"

Rather startled by his familiarity, the officer nonetheless replied good-naturedly, "Twenty-eight years."

The seaman nodded glumly. "Sucks, doesn't it?"

•

How can you tell if someone's a Green Beret?

He's the one jogging home after his vasectomy.

•

During an Army war game, the CO's jeep got stuck in the mud. Getting out and catching sight of a couple of privates lounging against a chain-link fence, the officer called them over to help extricate the jeep.

"Sorry, sir," one called back. "We've been classified dead and are under orders not to participate in any maneuvers."

The officer nodded grimly, turned to his driver, and barked, "Throw some of those corpses under the rear wheels for traction, Sergeant!"

An Army Air Corps student pilot was thrilled when she made her first perfectly smooth landing. Her elation turned to panic, however, when she stepped on the brakes and nothing happened. "The brakes have failed!" she screamed, turning white as a sheet.

"I'm not surprised," commented the flight instructor drily. "We're still two feet off the ground."

•

What's the definition of "military intelligence"?

An officer who thinks "cooking" and "screwing" are two cities in China.

•

At a veteran's meeting in Washington, DC, a corporal was approached by a scruffy fellow. "You don't remember me, do you, Harris?" he asked belligerently. Unsatisfied with the officer's assurances, the veteran demanded, "So where was I? What did I do?"

"You were a company clerk at Andrews Air Force Base," replied the officer crisply, "and you didn't do shit."

"I'll be damned," exclaimed the veteran, a smile spreading across his face. "You *do* remember me!"

•

"Mommy, what are these?" The four-year-old came into the kitchen with a find from her parents' bureau drawer.

"Those are Daddy's dog tags, Samantha."

"But Mommy," asked the puzzled child, "when was Daddy a dog?"

•

Did you hear about the terrorist who tried to blow up an Israeli bus?

He burned his lips on the exhaust pipe.

•

Early in his Air Force training, the young flier tried to impress the instructor with his knowledge of aeronautics. Visibly bored, the seasoned instructor dismissed his technical talk with a wave.

"Listen up, buddy—this is all you need to know," he drawled. "When you push on this stick, the trees get bigger. When you pull back, they get smaller. Hold it there, and they'll get bigger again."

•

What's the difference between a prophylactic and an Army-issue parachute?

When the parachute fails, somebody *dies*.

•

"Just like the movies, eh?" said the seasoned veteran to the new recruit sharing his foxhole, as artillery boomed and tracers lit the steamy jungle sky.

"Yeah," agreed the fellow, flinching as a shell exploded a few yards away, "but now's the part when I take my popcorn, leave the theater and go home."

•

The Marine unit was being transferred to quarters aboard a new ship, and amidst the bustle of activity a huge cast-iron safe stood on the foredeck. Finally a Marine sentry took up his position next to it, provoking an irate outburst from the embarkation officer. "Goddamn it, Hernandez—you are under orders not to let that safe out of your sight long enough to blink!"

"Yes sir, I know sir," Hernandez agreed cheerfully. "But anyone strong enough to move that safe isn't someone I'd fuck with anyhow, sir."

•

Did you hear about the NCO who was half Irish and half Italian?

He gave himself an order he couldn't understand.

•

Having passed the induction physical with flying colors, Garcia went on to that part of the exam which appraised his mental state. "Can you tell me why you want to join the Navy?" asked the psychologist.

"My father said it'd be a good idea," was Garcia's frank answer.

"I see." The psychologist made a note on his chart. "And what does your father do?"

"He's in the Army."

•

What's six inches long, has a bald head, and drives WACs crazy?

A one-hundred dollar bill.

•

The Navy chaplain was nervous about performing his first funeral service, but the undertaker promised to assist him, and in due course whispered, "Now it's time to instruct the family to come up and view the body."

The chaplain cleared his throat. "Will the family of the deceased please come forward now and pass around the bier?" he asked, then turned beet-red at his unfortunate choice of words. There was no comment, though, and the chaplain began to think he'd gotten away with it until he overheard one cemetery worker complain to another, "I didn't get any beer—did you?"

"Didn't you hear the chaplain?" asked the other guy. "It was just for the family."

•

Why did the drill instructor go around with his fly open?

Just in case he had to count to eleven.

The captain posted to a small Air Force radar site was noted for being a real stickler. Coming to inform Sergeant Bryce of a staff meeting, he was infuriated to find him leaning back in his chair with his feet up on the desk. "Sergeant Bryce, you are displaying abominable military bearing and deportment," the captain scolded. "Think of the Air Force image! Think of the morale of your men!"

Duly chastised, Bryce followed the captain down the hall to the commander's office—where the CO was leaning back, feet up on his desk.

Bryce turned to the captain and asked in a loud whisper, "Well, sir, do you want to tell him, or is it up to me?"

•

How come Polish enlisted men never become medics? They can't fit the little bottles into the typewriter.

•

The Airborne Army major was used to harassment from Air Force fliers about crazy Army paratroopers jumping out of perfectly good aircraft. "Obviously the Air Force knows there's no such thing as a 'perfectly good aircraft,'" the irritated major finally countered one afternoon, "because they pay you bastards four times as much to stay in one as the Army pays its men to jump."

"You've got it all wrong, Major," an Air Force sergeant replied. "The Army figures anyone stupid enough to jump out of an airplane voluntarily is gonna be too dumb to bitch about the salary."

•

Why do they call camels ships of the desert?
Because they're full of Iraqi seamen.

•

Two drill sergeants were standing outside the PX bitching about the long hours. "This job works me so damn hard," complained Meade, "that even making love to my wife is getting to feel like a chore."

"No way could that be considered work," objected Daly. They argued the point back and forth and finally agreed to turn the question over to the next person to come out of the PX. This happened to be Perkins, a private in Daly's platoon.

"Tell me, soldier," began Meade, "if you got up every day at 5 A.M., worked your ass off for 18 hours, went home, prepared your gear for the next day, and fell into bed, would making love be a pleasure or a duty?"

Perkins scratched his head. "I'd have to say it would be a pleasure, sir," he finally replied.

"And why is that?"

"Because if it were work, Sergeant Daly would have me doing it already."

•

Kramer enlisted in the Army but hadn't really come to terms with his non-civilian status. A few weeks into his service, he requested a weekend pass in order to be present at his sister's wedding. When twenty-four hours' leave was granted, Kramer protested vehemently. "You don't understand, sir—I'm *in* the wedding."

"No, *you* don't understand," the top sergeant assured him calmly. "You're *in* the Army."

•

What do you call a black woman in the Army?
A WACoon.

•

Observing a first lieutenant struggling for forty-five minutes to repair a flat tire on his Jeep, the motorpool sergeant came over with a small torch, heated the lug nuts briefly, and unscrewed them with ease.

He dismissed the lieutenant's curt thanks with a wave. "You just have to be smarter than it is, sir."

•

During training exercises, the lieutenant driving down a muddy back road encountered another car stuck in the mud, a red-faced major at the wheel. "Your Jeep stuck, sir?" asked the lieutenant cheerfully as he pulled alongside.

"Nope," replied the major, coming over and handing him the keys. "Yours is."

•

A tourist in Fairbanks noticed a native woman with a blonde-haired, blue-eyed baby in a sling on her back. Asking permission to take her picture, the tourist asked, "Is your child a full-blooded Eskimo?"

"Half," replied the young mother, snorting at the dumb question.

"Half what?" pursued the tourist. "Half-English? Half-Scandinavian, maybe?"

The woman shrugged. "Half-Coast Guard."

After a week in a remote Foreign Legion outpost in the Sahara, the recruit screwed up his nerve and asked the corporal what the men did for recreation. "Wait till Friday," counseled the officer.

"Sir, there's almost a hundred men here, and there can't be more than five women in the nearest village . . . which is two days away," pursued the soldier unhappily.

"Wait till Friday."

So on Friday the private watched carefully as a huge herd of camels was herded into the encampment. At a signal the troops seemed to go wild, slugging and trampling over each other in their haste to begin screwing the camels. Catching sight of the corporal racing past, the recruit grabbed him by the arm. "Why the rush?" he asked. "There must be over three hundred camels to go around."

The corporal looked incredulous. "You want to get stuck with an ugly one?"

•

Did you hear about the big sale of surplus Venetian blinds to the Ethiopian Army?

It's using them for bunk beds.

Little Freddy was playing airplane with a cardboard box in his back yard. *"Vroom, vroom,* rat-a-tat-a-tat," he yelled happily. "Here I am, a real U.S. Army pilot, flying at thirty thousand feet." Little Louise looked over the fence and called, "Can I play too?"

"Sure you can," called out the little boy, adjusting his goggles. "Lemme bring her in nice and slow like a real Army pilot and I'll take you up for a spin."

Louise climbed in behind him. "Fasten your seatbelt," ordered the boy, checking his imaginary gauges and roaring like a jet engine. "I'm a real Army pilot, so prepare for take-off." The little girl squealed in excitement as the plane roared through imaginary clouds and flawlessly performed imaginary barrel rolls. But as soon as they reached cruising altitude, she announced she had to pee.

"Can't scrub the mission," announced Freddy matter-of-factly. "You'll have to hold it, soldier." But in a few minutes he looked down and noticed a yellow stream trickling through the cockpit. Following it back, he observed with fascination its origin in little Louise's snatch. "Can I touch it?" he asked.

Louise nodded.

"Nice," he commented suavely.

"Would you like to kiss it?" she asked coyly.

"Gee," stammered Freddy, "I'm not a *real* Army pilot, you know."

What would a JAP in the Army Reserve do during a nuclear holocaust?

Run for her sun reflector.

•

A man was walking down a street in Belfast late one night when a shadowy figure, face obscured by a ski mask, stepped out in front of him. "Halt!" the soldier called, blocking his path with an automatic rifle. "Are you Catholic or Protestant?"

The passerby wiped the sweat off his brow. "Neither," he replied with a sigh of relief. "I'm Jewish."

The gunman pulled the trigger and blasted his victim to smithereens. Turning away with a grin, he remarked, "I must be the luckiest Arab in Ireland tonight."

•

What do you call a general in the Italian Army with a big dick?

Genitalia.

The Navy lawyer marched into the brig and announced that she had some good news and some bad news.

"What's the bad news?" asked the hulking private, who'd been found guilty of bludgeoning an inoffensive ensign to death.

"The provost marshal refuses to issue a stay of execution."

The prisoner paled and collapsed onto his bunk. "What's the good news?"

The lawyer flashed him an encouraging smile. "I got your voltage reduced."

•

How can you tell when a helicopter's been built for the Polish Army?

The pilot's chair is an ejection seat.

•

Did you hear about the Italian Navy's tragic accident?

A hundred and thirty-seven sailors drowned trying to push-start their new submarine.

Pfc Tunley counted the days, the weeks, the hours, until she went off-duty for weekend leave and her hunky fiancé picked her up at the gate. The time sped by all too fast, and Sunday night she cabled her duty station: MASSIVE SNOWSTORM, ROADS BLOCKED. REQUEST EXTENSION.

The reply arrived minutes later. EXTENSION GRANTED. BRING PHOTOGRAPHS.

•

Hear about the Iranian mine detector?

He puts his hand over his ears and walks forward, tapping his foot.

•

Not being the least bit athletically inclined, the new recruit was having a hell of a time in boot camp. One morning she made it as far as the obstacle course but soon fell to the ground, clutching her ankle. "What's the matter, soldier?" barked the sergeant, looking down sternly.

"Sir, it's my leg . . . I think I've broken a bone."

"Well don't just lie there," he snapped. "Start doing push-ups."

•

How does an Iranian firing squad line up?
One behind the other.

•

The handsome Marine considered himself quite the stud, and indeed had no trouble persuading the good-looking sergeant to come back to his apartment. After making love to her, he rolled over and lit a cigarette. His self-satisfied smile vanished, however, when the woman hopped out of bed and declared, "You may look like Mel Gibson, but you're lousy in the sack."

The indignant Marine snapped, "I don't see what makes you such an expert after only forty-five seconds!"

•

What happened in the Middle East following Iraq's invasion of Kuwait?

An hour later Switzerland declared itself neutral and Italy surrendered.

●

Two Marines got off guard duty and decided to head into town for a quick drink. As they approached a street light, Malone looked over and whistled admiringly. "Quite a bulge you've got in your pants, Mancini."

"The only place in town serving drinks this late is a gay bar," the soldier explained curtly.

"So, you looking for some action?" his buddy teased. "What's with the bulge?"

Mancini snarled, "I stuffed two handgrenades in my shorts. First queer that tries to feel me up gets his hand blown off."

●

Two Palestinian commandos were driving through downtown Tel Aviv when the white-faced driver turned and asked nervously, "Hassan—what happens if the bomb in the back seat detonates before we reach the embassy?"

"Calm down, Khalid," soothed his partner. "I have a back-up in the trunk."

•

Why was the performance of the Italian Army during World War II so deplorable?

When the soldiers cabled from the front for shells, the munitions officers sent them ziti.

•

What's the new Iraqi Army flag?

A white cross on a white background.

•

Captain Harding met with Sergeant Fry to inform him that a special man was needed for an extremely perilous mission. "It involves parachuting at night into heavily populated enemy territory," the captain explained, "so the soldier must be extraordinarily brave, utterly dependable, and have nerves of steel—"

"Say no more, sir," interrupted the sergeant. "Jackson is the man for the job."

"How can you be so sure? Have you seen him perform under fire?"

"I don't need to, Captain. Last week we showed the platoon that training film on VD—and Jackson ate strawberry shortcake right through the whole damn movie."

•

How do German soldiers tie their shoes?
  In Nazis.

•

Why does the new Italian Navy use glass-bottomed boats?
  So they can steer clear of the old Italian Navy.

•

Three privates were taken prisoner by the rebel forces, who decided to have them flogged to strike fear in their enemies. Not being a heartless beast, however, the rebel commander asked each man if he wished to have anything applied to his back to make the punishment more bearable.

Private DiFiore, whose parents hailed from the Old Country, requested olive oil. It was poured on his back and he was whipped within an inch of his life.

Next came Private Dunne, who prided himself on

being one tough son-of-a-bitch. "I need nothing," he declared, and was flogged till his back looked like hamburger.

Last came Private Feinstein, who had paid close attention. When the commander asked what he would like on his back, Feinstein replied, "Dunne."

•

Why do female paratroopers wear jockstraps?
So they don't whistle on the way down.

•

How can you identify a Rumanian jet fighter in a snowstorm?
It's the one with chains on the propellers.

•

The three British soldiers were taken prisoner by a Burmese hill tribe and brought before the native chief. "You have a choice," he announced, pointing his spear at the first man. "Death or *minanda*?"

"Jolly good," said the first soldier. *"Minanda."*

He was seized and viciously sodomized by the entire tribe, after which the chief stepped over his bleeding body and turned to the second Brit. "And you?"

The trembling fellow whispered, *"Minanda."* He, too, was abused by every man in the tribe, which then turned eagerly to the third soldier, who stood quaking in fear.

"Death or *minanda*?"

Throgmorton straightened up and looked him straight in the eye. "Death."

"Excellent!" said the chief. "Death by *minanda*!"

•

What's the safest place in a Marine barracks to hide your money?

Under the soap.

•

Did you hear about the aerial reconnaissance expert who didn't believe in flying saucers . . .

. . . until he pinched a waitress in a coffee shop?

•

The overweight wife of a Marine drill instructor took up jogging, running a circuit around the base. Each morning she would encounter the same platoon, and she got into the habit of running in tempo with their cadence calls.

After a few weeks she was able to keep up with them, and not too much later was actually able to overtake them. But the real hallmark of her progress came one morning when she heard as she ran by, "The DI's big wife used to dine/ But now she's lookin' mighty fine."

•

"Nein! Nein!" shrieked the pretty German *fräulein,* cornered by ten Russian soldiers in a dark alley during the invasion of Berlin.

So one of the Russians left.

•

Putney had joined the Army Airborne with dreams of parachuting, but now that the moment had come for his first jump, he was pretty scared. The instructor assured him that all he had to do was count to ten and pull the cord. "Relax—even if your chute malfunctions, the reserve will open automatically. And our truck will be waiting for you at the drop site."

With those comforting words, the instructor gave Putney a shove, and he found himself plummeting toward the earth.

After a few seconds of pure terror, the private began counting, and pulled the ripcord right on time. Nothing happened. Trying to stay calm, Putney waited for the reserve chute to open. Nothing happened. "Shit," he muttered as the ground rushed toward him, "I'll just bet the truck isn't there either."

•

Why doesn't the Army like volunteers who are half-German and half-Italian?

They attack suddenly, then surrender immediately.

•

What does a Pentagon general do with a fifty-thousand-dollar toilet seat?

Take fifty-thousand-dollar dumps.

•

Desperately clawing at his reserve chute, the Pfc was only 300 feet up and falling fast when he passed a

WAC coming up. "Know anything about parachutes?" he screamed frantically.

"Got me, soldier," she yelled as he plummeted past. "Know anything about dynamite?"

•

Why did the prostitute quit giving blowjobs and enlist in the Army as a computer programmer?

It involved a lot less down time.

•

What do you call a woman pilot with VD?

An aircraft carrier.

•

The gung-ho Green Beret went out on recon. Returning to base, he reported directly to the lieutenant and asked, "Are all the other men back?"

The lieutenant nodded. "All present and accounted for."

"No casualties?"

The lieutenant shook his head.

"Great!" exclaimed the Green Beret with a sign of relief. "Guess I *did* shoot a VC."

•

What do you call the grunt whose lower legs were blown off by a land mine?

Neil.

•

A grunt walked into a whorehouse in Tokyo, went up to the madam, and asked, "Do Oriental women really have horizontal pussies?"

"Why?" asked the madam. "Are you harmonica player?"

•

Why's Nelson Mandela like an old World War II K-ration?

They've both spent a long, long time in the can.

•

What was the name of the Roman soldier who nailed Jesus to the cross?

Spike.

•

Duane and Dougie, both privates from the same little town in Louisiana, got a weekend furlough and couldn't wait to go fishing. They rented a boat and spent the whole afternoon reeling in bass. When the sun began to go down, Duane wondered out loud whether there was some way the spot could be marked so they could find it again the next day.

"I know!" Dougie cried. "I'll put an X on the bottom of the boat."

"You shit-for-brains," snorted his buddy scornfully. "That is the stupidest idea I ever heard. How do you know we'll get the same boat tomorrow?"

•

Why couldn't the WAVE get pregnant during the gale at sea?

The seamen kept falling to the floor.

•

What do the German Army and Roseanne Barr have in common?

They both lost the Battle of the Bulge.

•

Two NCOs stationed in Hawaii went down to the beach for some R&R. They waded into the surf when one yelped, "A crab bit one of my toes!"

"Which one?" asked her companion, following her back up onto the beach.

"How should I know?" she screeched. "All crabs look alike."

•

Halfway through World War II Adolf Hitler consulted a clairvoyant to find out on what day he would die. He almost fell off his little gilt chair when she informed him that his death would fall on a Jewish holiday.

"Me—impossible!" protested the corporal. "Which Jewish holiday?"

"Mein Führer," the clairvoyant pointed out, *"any* day you die will be a Jewish holiday."

•

How do you make Chicken Vietnam?

First you napalm a chicken farm. . . .

•

The drill sergeant lost no time endearing himself to his new bunch of recruits. Walking down the center aisle of the barracks, he bellowed at the boys on his right, "You're all shit-ass, good-for-nothing excuses for men."

Turning to the ones on his left, he howled, "And *you* limp-wristed cocksuckers are the sorriest sons-of-bitches I've ever set eyes on!"

When a meek-looking man got to his feet, the DI spun around to confront him. "You gotta problem?" he demanded belligerently.

"Oh, no sir," replied the new recruit timidly. "It's just that I'm on the wrong side of the room."

•

What's Kurt Waldheimer Disease?

It's like Alzheimer's Disease, except you only forget your war crimes.

•

What do you call a WAC who can suck a golf ball through fifty feet of garden hose?

Darling.

•

In the early fifties the first true computer came on the market, but it was so expensive that only the U.S. Government could afford one. The machine was so big that an annex to the Pentagon had to be built to house it, but the military was immensely proud of its new acquisition and couldn't wait to try out its gleaming rows of dials and buttons.

General MacIntyre suggested the computer run a mock military engagement, and his colleagues loved the idea. They programmed the machine with every conceivable factor: troop strength and equipment, terrain, climate, enemy position, season and time of day, psychological variables, and so on. This alone took days, but finally the generals gathered around as the programmer typed in the first question: "Should our forces attack by sea from the south-south-east, or by air from due east?"

Lights blinked, circuits hummed, and the Joint Chiefs of Staff waited in respectful silence for what seemed like hours. Finally a print-out emerged from the console, and the generals jumped up. "Yes," it read.

"Yes, what?!?" bellowed MacIntyre.

Lights blinked rapidly, and the computer replied, "Yes, *sir*!"

•

What was the motto of the Greek troops who fought in the Falkland Islands conflict?
  "Save the Sheep!"

•

How can you spot the latest Italian fighter-bomber?
  It's got a pointy nose and hair under its wings.

•

What's the difference between a Libyan terrorist and a JAP?
  A terrorist makes fewer demands.

•

What's the definition of a virgin El Salvador soldier?
  One who hasn't raped a nun yet.

Sergeant Wohl, an Army systems engineer, showed such technical aptitude that he was soon in charge of the master control room of the entire North American DEW system. And it was Wohl who was asked to demonstrate the efficacy and capability of the system to a visiting five-star general.

Wohl saluted the officer, then turned to his console and began deftly flipping switches, consulting printouts, and inputting instructions. Suddenly smoke poured out of the vents, computer tape spewed forth, lights flickered and went out, and the visiting party was left in the dark—as was most of the continental US.

Trying to stay cool, Wohl's commanding officer asked, "Sergeant Wohl, what the hell are you going to do now?"

The white-faced soldier replied, "I'm going to buy a small farm in Iowa, sir!"

•

Did you hear what happened when Poland finally got involved in the war against Iraq and sent four thousand soldiers to the Gulf?

Mexico didn't know what to do with 'em.

During basic training, the soldiers were policing the grounds in front of the barracks when a platoon of WACs came by. The privates straightened up and looked the women over hungrily, and the WACs couldn't resist getting an eyeful themselves.

That was enough for their drill sergeant. Ordering the women to stand at attention facing the barracks, she instructed the red-faced platoon to take a good look. "There are six hundred miles of dick on this base," she bellowed, "and let me make one thing perfectly clear: you girls aren't getting an inch of it."

Did you hear the Polish government bought a thousand septic tanks?

As soon as they learn how to drive them, they're going to invade the Soviet Union.

A local entrepreneur was delighted when the Army decided to build a new base outside the little town. He set up a little whorehouse and soon was making good money. The only problem was the shortage of local talent—there weren't enough girls to satisfy the demand. Unhappy at the thought of the lost revenue, especially with the weekend coming up, the enterprising fellow drove to the city, bought several inflatable fuck dolls, and set them up in his upstairs rooms. Since his clientele consisted largely of wet-behind-the-ears farm boys, he figured they'd never know the difference. He ushered his first customer into a room housing one of the new lovelies, confidently assuring the private he was in for an especially good time.

When the GI came out a little while later, the manager was waiting curiously in the hallway. "Well, how'd you like the new girl?" he asked with a lewd wink.

"I don't know what happened," admitted the soldier ruefully, scratching his head. "I bit her on the tit, she farted, and flew out the window."

•

What do Saddam Hussein and pantyhose have in common?

They both rub Bush the wrong way.

•

Maloney and McGuire, hunting buddies since boyhood, enlisted together and swore a blood oath that neither would desert the other on the field of battle. And indeed the fateful day came when an artillery shell exploded nearby, gravely wounding McGuire.

Remembering his oath, Maloney took a deep breath, scrambled across the muddy field under heavy fire, dragged his buddy back to his foxhole, and ministered to him until the medic finally arrived. "Well Doc, is he going to make it?" he asked, tears streaking his grimy face.

"It's a tough call, Private," conceded the doctor. "He'd have a better chance if you hadn't gutted him first."

•

How do you find a foxhole?
  Lift its tail.

•

The Italian and the Polish paratroopers were arguing about who was best at folding his parachute. Unable to resolve their dispute on the ground, they decided to go up in a plane and judge by the mid-air performance of the chutes. The Polish soldier jumped first, pulled the cord, and grinned as the wind filled his chute and he began floating gently toward the landing zone. The Italian jumped, pulled the ripcord—and nothing happened. He pulled the safety cord—and nothing happened. And in a matter of seconds he plummeted like a stone past the other parachutist.

"Oh," yelled the Pole indignantly, yanking off his harness, "so you wanna *race!*"

·

What do you get when you cross a Hispanic soldier with an Iraqi one?

Oil of Olé.

·

When the three reservists were called to active duty for Operation Desert Shield, each was instructed to bring appropriate equipment for survival. The duty sergeant nodded approvingly at McClosky's canteen. "I'm gonna sweat plenty under that desert sun, and I'll need extra fluid," the fellow explained.

Montefiore held up the big pot of pasta he was carrying. "Itsa hungry work, marching through sand. Louisa's spaghetti alla marinara will keepa my strength up."

The sergeant shrugged and turned to the third soldier, who was shouldering the front door of a '57 Chevy.

"I've read up on the place, and it's hot as hell,"

explained Kosinski with a knowledgeable look. "I want to be able to roll down the window."

•

Did you hear they divided Baghdad into two sections?

Smoking and Non-Smoking.

•

The officer ordered a beer and sized up the small-town bar, quickly picking out the best-looking woman in the place. He took a seat next to her, pulled a frog out of his pocket, and asked if he could buy her a drink. "I'm Lieutenant Bishop and this is Charlie," he said suavely. "He's a very special frog."

"Oh yeah? How come?" she asked skeptically.

The lieutenant was reluctant to tell her, but finally leaned over and whispered, "This frog can eat pussy."

The girl slapped him, and called him a pig and a filthy liar to boot. But no, the guy assured her, it was really true—Charlie was one talented frog. And after much back and forth and a couple of drinks, the woman's curiosity got the better of her and she invited him back to her place so she could see for herself.

The lieutenant placed the frog carefully between her thighs, and ordered, "Okay Charlie, do your stuff!"

The frog just sat there.

"C'mon Charlie, hit it!" ordered his owner.

The frog just sat there.

The man sighed and with a resigned expression picked up the frog. "Charlie, this is the last time I'm going to show you."

●

Why do Iraqi pilots learn to fly in half the time?

They don't have to learn how to land.

●

A man was having a few when he noticed a sailor at the other end of the bar. The sailor had a completely normal physique except for one thing: his head was tiny, about the size of an orange. After a few drinks, the fellow screwed up his courage and asked the obvious question.

The sailor took it in good humor, explaining that some time ago his destroyer had been torpedoed in the Pacific. "I came to on this beautiful little beach, and I heard this sad little whimpering sound coming from behind some rocks. It turned out to be a mermaid, who was so grateful when I carried her back to the water's edge that she promised to grant me any three wishes. Well, as you can imagine, my first wish was to get home safely."

The sailor took a slug of his beer and continued. "Suddenly a ship appeared on the horizon, heading my way, so my next wish was to be incredibly rich. And—wham!—a trunk full of jewels and gold coins appeared right next to me on the beach. So then, being a red-blooded guy, I asked if we could make love.

" 'Take a look,' she said, 'and you'll see I'm not built for that sort of thing.'

"Okay," I said, "so how about a little head?"

•

If you think old soldiers fade away—

. . . you should see one trying to get into an old uniform.

•

Hear about the ad for Swiss Army rifles?

"Never been shot—only dropped once."

•

87

Six-year-old Joey and eight-year-old Mikey were thrilled when their Daddy, a Marine corporal, came home on leave, and especially by the salty language that now filled the air. "You say 'ass,'" instructed Mikey on the way down to breakfast, "and I'll say 'hell.'"

All excited by their plan, they trooped downstairs, where their mother asked them what they wanted for breakfast. "Aw, hell," blustered Mikey, "gimme some Cheerios." His mother slapped him off his stool and sent him bawling to his room, then turned to Joey. "How about you?"

"I dunno," quavered the six-year-old, "but you can bet your ass it ain't gonna be Cheerios."

•

How do you sink the Iraqi Navy?
   Put it in water.

•

Unaware of the other's presence, an Arab in his tank and an Israeli in his are motoring up opposite sides of the same hill. They reach the top at precisely the same moment, and the tanks collide with a tremendous crash.

The Arab climbs quickly out of the turret of his vehicle, arms raised in a gesture of surrender.

Just as quickly, the Israeli leaps from his tank, screaming, "WHIPLASH!"

•

What's the motto of the Greek Army?

"Never Leave Your Buddy's Behind."

•

The two inexperienced GIs were goggle-eyed during their first overseas crossing. "Gosh, that's the most water I ever saw in my whole life," admitted the first guy, who came from Idaho. "How about you?"

"Aw, you ain't seen nothin' yet," said his buddy, playing it cool. "That's only the top of it."

•

The Navy is what you join to see the world—
. . . and then you spend two years in a submarine.

•

Didrickson lined up for his first Army sick call. While he was waiting for his name to be called, the private to his left leaned over and said conspiratorially, "I hear these doctors are really tough. They don't want any malingerers, you know. A guy in my unit came in complaining about his corns, and the surgeon cut three toes off."

Didrickson blanched, and turned even paler when the guy on his right nodded in confirmation. "Listen to *this*: a guy in my barracks came in with an earache and came back with a bandage where his ear used to be."

That did it. The new recruit jumped to his feet and yelped, "I've gotta get out of here—I've got the clap!"

.

Young Jose never quite got over his miserable childhood as an orphan in the ghetto. When he turned eighteen he joined the Army, but old habits die hard, and one night the sergeant found him rummaging around the garbage and eating out of the discarded cans and jars.

"On your feet, Hernandez," he bellowed. "You'll eat in the mess hall—you're no better than the rest of us."

.

The draft board has a special method for testing male enlistees. They offer them a date with either of two women, one beautiful and the other homely.

If a guy goes for the good-looking one, the Army takes him.

If he goes for the homely one, the Army rejects him.

If he rejects both, he gets sent over to the Navy recruiting station.

•

How does a French soldier make love?

He kisses both his wife's cheeks before he moves to the front.

•

Gustafson's mother died during basic training, and it was the company sergeant's duty to inform him. Tact had never been one of Sergeant Marek's strong suits, and that afternoon he went into the barracks, called the soldier over and said, "Gustafson, your mother's dead."

Of course the shock caused the poor guy to break down completely, and he had to be dismissed from active duty for quite a while. The sergeant's bluntness was the topic of considerable discussion, and not long afterward his superior officer summoned him in for a little talk. "When you deliver personal news of this sort," the corporal admonished, "it's important not to be quite so . . . uh . . . direct about it. Next time break it a little more gradually."

Marek assured him he'd try to be more sensitive. And as luck would have it, another soldier's father was killed in a car accident later that same week. This time Marek lined up the platoon outside the barracks, and took a deep breath. "Everyone whose father is still alive, take one step forward," he ordered. *"Not* so fast, Fredericks."

•

At the conclusion of the commanding general's inspection of the post's mess facilities, he turned to one of the recruits and asked jovially, "How's the food here?"

"We fight over it all the time, sir," was the reply.

The general beamed. "That good, eh?"

"Not exactly, sir. The loser has to eat it."

•

What's the definition of slow dancing?

A naval engagement without the loss of seamen.

Sergeant Major Guthrie walked to the back of the Glasgow pharmacy and showed the chief pharmacist a condom, clearly worn out from numerous engagements. "How much, mon, to repair this prophylactic?"

The druggist shook his head. "Well, I could sterilize it, put a new elastic around the base, maybe patch the spot near the tip where it's wearing thin . . . but by that time it'd cost you less just to buy a new one."

Guthrie winced, and said he'd have to think it over. The next day he came back into the pharmacy and announced with a smile, "The regiment has voted to replace."

What's green and takes off from Berlin?
Snotzies.

Did you hear what happened to the fly on the latrine seat?
It got pissed off.

Private Harris was sent home from the front with a shrapnel wound, and ended up losing one ball. Nevertheless he met a lovely young nurse in the hospital, fell in love, and was thrilled when she agreed to marry him. He assumed that she was a virgin, and when the wedding night revealed otherwise, he lost his temper and started yelling at her.

Finally the bride retorted, "You're missing something too, and I'm not making a federal case out of it, now am I?"

"That's a cheap shot," howled the vet. "My enemies did this to me!"

"Big deal," she returned. "My friends did this to me!"

•

Why did the promiscuous girl have legs like the United States Army?

They were open to any man between the ages of 18 and 35.

•

The notoriously tough sergeant major was inspecting the barracks when he overheard one terrified recruit whisper, "Sergeant Major Adams has the heart of a tiny child . . . on his desk . . . in a jar."

Without missing a beat, Adams snarled, "Damned if they don't find out every little thing about you."

•

Clark telephoned the Military Police and informed the desk sergeant that he'd been getting threatening letters. "Isn't that against the law?" he blustered.

"It certainly is," replied the MP. "Have you any idea who the sender is?"

"Yeah," Clark admitted, "my girlfriend's husband."

•

What goes "hop, skip, jump, ka-blam!"?
Kuwaiti children playing in a minefield.

•

Boot camp required all the recruits to pass a basic swimming test, and Bennett, who'd never been more than ankle-deep in a creek, was utterly terrified. After much gasping and floundering, she finally learned to dog-paddle well enough for the kind-hearted instructor to pass her—with the following instructions should she ever find herself aboard a sinking ship: "Abandon your battle station, take a running jump overboard, go straight to the bottom, and run as fast as you can."

•

Simpson had always refused to believe the stories about Sergeant Boll's sadistic streak. And when he heard Boll begin to describe a prostitute he'd encountered, Simpson was glad he'd given his fellow sergeant the benefit of the doubt. "She was so young— couldn't have been more than fifteen—and thin as a rail," began Boll, a sad look coming over his grizzled face. "It was a cold night, but she was only wearing a shawl over a thin cotton dress. She must have been starving, and her arms and legs were like broomsticks, and cold to the touch. "In fact," he continued, "I could hardly hold back the tears while I was screwing her."

•

Ensign Brown had wanted to serve on a submarine since childhood, and couldn't wait to impress the coxswain with the extent of his expertise. The coxswain, however, cut his enthusiastic speech short with the golden rule of submarine service: "Just count how many times we dive, add the number of times we surface, and divide by two. If it doesn't come out even, don't open the hatch."

•

How did the Germans capture Poland so easily?

They marched in backwards and said they were leaving.

•

"Did you say you'd cooked before?" the major asked the new chief cook.

"Oh, yes sir," the cook replied, "in the officers' mess. Wounded twice."

"You're a very lucky man," the major commented sincerely. "I'm amazed they didn't kill you."

•

The C-130 was cruising at twelve hundred feet, and each of the novice jumpers was listening very carefully to the sergeant's explanation of how to operate the reserve chute in case of an emergency. "Snap back immediately into a tight body position," he instructed, yelling against the roar of the engines. "Then pull the reserve chute's ripcord and it'll open."

A white-faced private raised his hand. "Sir, if my main parachute doesn't open, how long do I have to pull my reserve?

"The rest of your life," the sergeant replied earnestly, "the rest of your life."

•

After a few weeks in the remote Foreign Legion outpost, young Pierre was horny enough to ask a fellow soldier what was available in the way of sex. "The camels come every Friday," Private LeJeune explained.

"Camels!" Pierre recoiled in shock, disgusted by his companion's tastes. A few more lonely weeks brought him around, however, and not long afterwards he found himself counting the hours on a Friday afternoon. No sooner had the camels come through the gate than the young soldier had gotten into position and began pumping away.

"Pierre, Pierre, what in God's name are you doing?" called LeJeune, running up and grabbing him.

"See for yourself," yelled the furious soldier. "You told me I had to wait for Friday."

"Yes, yes, but the camels are to take us to the whorehouse in town!"

•

What's one idea that never got off the ground?
The Polish Air Force.

•

The irascible guard was not at all happy to see Hawkins pull up at the gate with one arm firmly around his affectionate date's shoulders. "Next time you come through this checkpoint I expect you to use *both* hands!"

"Okay, sir," responded the Marine obediently, "but how do you expect me to steer?"

•

Why's an Italian tank like an Italian girl?
On a cold morning when you really need it, it won't kick over.

Why shouldn't you eat at a restaurant run by the PLO?

They don't take orders, they just make demands.

•

Ensign Monteverdi was at sea when his wife gave birth to twins. He was pretty annoyed to find out his brother had taken the liberty of naming the children in his absence. "Some nerve!" he commented bitterly. "So what name did he pick for my daughter?"

"Denise," replied his wife.

"Not too bad," the sailor admitted. "I can live with that. And for the boy?"

"Da nephew."

•

Why was the gay sergeant kicked out of the service?

He was found playing with his privates.

•

A platoon of Green Berets was temporarily billeted near a select women's college. The commanding officer immediately made an appointment with the dean of students to alert her to the dangers of the situation. "My men have been out on maneuvers for over six months and are pretty damn . . . uh, hungry for female companionship," he informed her. "I advise that you lock the dorms at night and keep the campus gates guarded at all times."

"May I remind you of the extraordinary reputation of the College of the Sacred Heart?" responded the dean condescendingly. "Our girls have it up here." And she tapped her temple with her index finger.

"If you say so, ma'am," said the colonel politely. "But let me assure you that it makes no difference where they have it—my men will find it."

●

What happened when all the men in the leper colony enlisted?

They were defeeted.

Then what?

They were disarmed.

●

Two Navy pilots were shot down in the Pacific and were bobbing along in a rubber raft when a Japanese submarine surfaced nearby. As one guy jumped to his feet and began waving frantically, the other cracked, "Yeah, that's the ticket—get up close and we'll ram him!"

•

The aviation cadet was being questioned by a veteran Airborne officer, who asked if he smoked, drank, or went out with loose women. "No, sir," was the sober young cadet's response to each inquiry.

"Well, why the hell do you want to study aviation?" asked the captain. "You've got your wings already."

•

The second lieutenant, putting his men through calisthenics and not paying much attention, called out, "Hips on shoulders, place." A look of confusion came over his face as he stopped to think, then to admit, "That can't be done. Hips, down."

•

Guard: Halt! Who goes there?
Rookie: Aw, you wouldn't know me. I just got here yesterday.

•

The general sent his helmet over to the utility section to have it varnished and polished. The GIs worked like maniacs, but the officer insisted on "more polish" on the steel, until the soldier in charge said apologetically, "That's as slick as we can get it, sir."

Just then a fly landed on the helmet, slid, and broke three legs. The general accepted the helmet.

•

Sign in ammo dump: IF YOU MUST SMOKE, GO AHEAD. THEN EXIT VIA THE HOLE WHICH WILL HAVE APPEARED IN THE ROOF.

•

At the USO show:
Pfc: Can you see the stage all right?
Pvt: Sure can.
Pfc: Is your seat comfortable?

Pvt: Oh, perfectly.
Pfc: It's not in the draft from the door?
Pvt: Nope.
Pfc: Great. Switch seats.

●

After a particularly brutal haircut, the GI took his revenge on the barber with a magic marker: on his nearly-bald skull, he wrote in big letters THIS END UP.

●

The typical no-nonsense sergeant was putting his new recruits through their first session of close-order drill. "Forward march!" he barked, then, in quick succession, "Halt!" "Right face!" "Forward march!" "About face!" "Left face!"

At that point one disgusted GI threw down his rifle and stalked off.

"And just where the hell do you think you're going?" bellowed the sergeant.

"I quit," was the disgusted reply. "No way am I marching off after some idiot who can't even make up his mind which way he's going."

●

Did you hear about the poor grunt who had insomnia so bad . . .

. . . he couldn't even sleep when it was time to get up?

•

Bus after bus came by, but the dim-witted private at the head of the line waved them past. Finally an irate woman at the end of the line yelled, "Hasn't your bus stopped *yet*, buddy?"

"Oh yes, several times," he called back. "But if I get on, I'll lose my place at the front of the line."

•

Sign in mess hall: FOOD WILL WIN THE WAR. Scrawled underneath: BUT HOW CAN WE GET THE ENEMY TO EAT HERE?

•

Did you hear about the absent-minded professor who enlisted in the paratroopers and became a lieutenant? He unbuckled his parachute, stepped out of the plane, counted to three . . . and pulled his rank.

Lieutenant: "Who the hell told you to put flowers on the corporal's desk?"
Private: "The corporal, sir."
Lieutenant: "Pretty, aren't they?"

•

Ever noticed there're two kinds of people in the Service?

Enlisted soldiers, and people with clothes that fit.

•

The British and the American sailors were discussing the capabilities of their respective aircraft carriers, and patriotic sentiments were running pretty deep. "The HMS *Indomitable* can do twenty-seven knots at flank speed," boasted the Brit. "What's your ship's top speed?"

"Can't say as I'm sure," drawled the American, "since we haven't opened her up yet. All she's been required to do so far is keep up with the planes."

•

Mrs. Smith met Mrs. Jones in the checkout line and asked how Herbie was doing in the Army.

"Oh, just fine, thanks," she replied proudly. "He's just been given AWOL, and next week they're going to make him a court-martial."

●

The new bride was waving and blowing kisses at the train, loaded with servicemen, that was heading for the front. As it pulled out of the station and began gathering speed, she suddenly paled. "Darling, wait!" she screamed at the top of her lungs. "I forgot to ask —what's our last name?"

●

The grim-faced medic reported that Franklin had swallowed his knife and that emergency surgery had failed to remove it.

"Fine, fine," said the distracted quartermaster. "Issue Franklin a new knife."

●

Lecturing a bunch of fresh faces at OCS, the officer asked them to consider the problem of having to raise a forty-foot flagpole with a squad of only ten men. A complicated discussion of blocks and tackles ensued, all of which the officer dismissed with a wave of his hand.

"The Army offers its officers a simple solution to this sort of logistical problem, gentlemen," he informed the class. "You say, 'Sergeant—get that flagpole up!' "

•

Remember how WACs used to blush at GI slang?
Now they memorize it.

•

At the Iraqi court-martial, the judge read the indictment, in which the defendant was accused of calling Saddam Hussein a dangerous lunatic. "You are charged with three crimes," he stated solemnly. "First, you have indulged in enemy propaganda. Second, you have libelled our Supreme Leader. And, third, you have betrayed a military secret."

•

108

Mess sergeant: "Hey, the guy next to you's working twice as fast as you are."

KP, gloomily: "I know—I talked to him about it, but he won't slow down."

•

The homesick sailor wrote home: "Mom, I joined the Navy because I was impressed with how clean and orderly the ships were kept. This week I learned who keeps them clean and orderly."

•

What do you call an Iraqi soldier with a sheep under one arm and a goat under the other?

Bisexual.

•

On the radio quiz show, the sailor was asked the difference between a blonde and a submarine. A long silence was broken by the MC urging the young fellow to think, and think fast.

Finally the embarrassed sailor gave up. "Sorry

about that," he apologized, "but I've never been out with a submarine."

•

Did you hear about the Vietnam draft dodger who claimed an exemption on the ground of bad eyesight . . .
    . . . and brought along his wife as evidence?

•

Did you hear about the Saddam Hussein condom?
It's for men who don't know when to pull out.

•

Did you hear about the corporal who was so well hung, he had to strap his dick to his leg?
Every time he spotted a pretty WAC, he kicked himself in the forehead.

•

The Navy pilot returned to the Japanese whorehouse in a state of great indignation. "I was here last week and caught a case of the clap!" he protested loudly.

"Toyota," replied the madam.

"What the hell does that mean, 'Toyota'?"

She replied with a smile, "You asked for it, you got it!"

•

Hear about the guy who's half black and half Japanese?

Every December 7th, he attacks Pearl Bailey.

•

Swensen grew up on a remote dairy farm in Minnesota, and one of the reasons he enlisted in the Army was to get some experience with women. He was posted overseas, and not long afterwards found himself a prostitute who was more than willing to initiate him into the mysteries of sex.

Undressing, she lay down and proceeded to instruct him carefully. "Stick it in, honey . . . all the way . . . now pull it out . . . okay, back in, slowly . . . more, oooh, more . . . now back out again—"

"For Christ's sake," interrupted the sweating GI, "could you make up your mind?"

Confucius say: Woman fighter pilot who flies plane upside-down has crack up.

•

A few weeks later Swensen found himself compelled to report to the infirmary, where he confessed, "Doc, I think I have V.D."

The medic instructed him to pull down his pants, and asked, "Does your dick burn after intercourse?"

"I dunno," admitted the confused private. "I didn't try to light it."

•

Did you hear about the WAVE stationed in San Diego who took her vibrator to the beach . . .
. . . so she could shake and bake?

•

Off duty for the afternoon, the GI stationed in Saudi Arabia decided to shop for a nice rug to ship back home. He headed into the bazaar and was soon accosted by a merchant who urged him to buy one of his fine Persian carpets. "Top quality, very good price," he promised the soldier. "You must buy one."

The soldier readily agreed that the rugs were beautiful and the prices good, but told the merchant there was a problem, "The rugs smell bad," he said frankly. "In fact, they stink."

"How dare you say that?" protested the Arab indignantly. "My carpets do not stink. *I* stink!"

●

The pilot's TBF fighter-bomber went down near a remote Pacific atoll, and it was twelve years before he was discovered and rescued. On the transport back to the States, he was asked what he'd like to have most, to which he replied, "After twelve years alone, you *know* what I want!"

So they took him straight to the whorehouse nearest the base. The pilot lost no time in undressing, putting on a condom, and stuffing wads of cotton in both ears and nostrils. "What on earth are you doing?" asked the puzzled hooker.

"If there's two things I hate," he explained curtly, "it's the sound of a woman screaming and the smell of burning rubber."

●

What do you call an Iraqi submarine captain?

Chicken of the Sea.

•

Why do so many French sailors like serving on submarines?

They love to go down. . . .

○

Ensign Phillips fancied himself quite the ladies' man, so when his ship was torpedoed and he found himself stranded on a desert island with six WAVEs, he couldn't believe his good fortune. They quickly agreed that each woman would have one night a week with the ensign. Phillips threw himself into the arrangement with gusto, working even on his day off, but as the weeks stretched into months, he found himself looking forward to that day of rest more and more eagerly.

One afternoon he was sitting on the beach and wishing for some more men to share his duties when he caught sight of a life raft bobbing in the waves. Phillips swam out to the guy, pulled the raft to shore, and did a little jig of happiness. "You can't believe how happy I am to see you," he cried.

The new fellow eyed him up and down and cooed,

"You're a sight for sore eyes, too, you gorgeous thing."

"Shit," sighed the ensign, "there go my Sundays."

•

What's the first rule of service in the Navy?

If it moves salute it; if it doesn't move, paint it.

•

The GI called his sweetheart from the base and told her he'd just gotten his orders. "I'm shipping out in two hours, honey, so just pull off those panties, spread your legs, and I'll be right over."

"Okay, Bobbie," said the obliging girl. "Want me to take my bra off, too?"

"Gina, I told you I'm in a hurry," he said exasperatedly. "No time to chew the fat."

•

How many Syrian arms experts does it take to screw in a light bulb?

Two. One to hold the bulb, and the other to ask the Soviet adviser which way to turn it.

Three soldiers, an American, a Russian, and an Egyptian, were cast away on a desert island. Time passed very slowly indeed, until a lovely woman swam ashore, wrapped in a flag which clung to her generous curves. "She's mine!" yelled the American, pointing to the red-white-and-blue of the cloth. He tore the flimsy covering off her, revealing red panties underneath.

"The red flag of the motherland," cried the Russian, saluting. "I claim her!" He elbowed the GI out of the way and tore off her panties.

The Egyptian cleared his throat and declared, "Ah, the beard of the Prophet . . ."

·

What does the Algerian infantryman call it when he catches syphillis at the oasis?

A French foreign lesion.

·

Every day the Israeli soldier at the checkpoint along the military highway would watch as an Arab rode by him on his donkey, his aged wife trudging before him. Finally, one day the soldier stopped him. "I've been watching you go by every morning for months," he commented, "and you always ride and your wife is always on foot. Why?"

"Wife no have donkey," replied the Arab with a shrug.

"I see. But why does she walk in front of you? Is that the custom of your people?"

The Arab shook his head. "Land mines."

•

Hear about the remodeled Iraqi tanks?

They have one speed in forward, and four in reverse.

•

Hodgkins was assigned guard duty from 2 A.M. till 6 A.M., and, try as he might, he couldn't keep his eyes open. And when he woke up, it was to the face of the officer of the day peering into the guard house window. Terrified of incurring his wrath, Hodgkins kept his head down and mumbled, ". . . and for another night passed in safety, we thank you, Lord." Then he sat up and cried fervently, "AMEN!"

Did you hear about the new pen the Pentagon just perfected for the Gulf war?

It writes under sand.

•

The Kuwaiti platoon was plagued with skin problems, so the officer in charge finally sought the advice of an American medic. Returning, he called his men together and informed him that the cause of the problem was poor hygiene.

"From now on, we will change our underwear on a regular basis," he announced decisively. "Tariq, you will change with Mohammed . . . Mohammed, change underwear with Abdul . . ."

•

Why don't Iraqis go to bars anymore?

They can get bombed at home.

MEN AND WOMEN OF THE ARMED FORCES

If you'd like to see your favorite military joke in print, please send it to:

Blanche Knott
c/o St. Martin's Press
175 Fifth Avenue
New York, N.Y. 10010

We cannot offer compensation, but will do our best to see that your name and outfit are credited in our next military book—if you dare!

READ

MY

LIPS.

The Wit & Wisdom of

GEORGE
BUSH

With some reflections by Dan Quayle
edited by Ken Brady & Jeremy Solomon

THE WIT & WISDOM OF GEORGE BUSH
Brady & Solomon, eds.
_____ **91687-6 $2.95 U.S.**   _____ **91688-4 $3.95 Can.**